Northern Stage in association with Soho Theatre presents

OH, THE HUMANITY
AND OTHER GOOD INTENTIONS
By Will Eno

Oh, The Humanity and other good intentions had its
world premiere on 9 September 2011 at Northern Stage
in Newcastle.

Northern Stage is supported by Arts Council England
and Newcastle City Council.

Soho Theatre is supported by Arts Council England
and Westminster Council.

Registered Charity No: 267334

Supported using public funding by
**ARTS COUNCIL
ENGLAND**

A NOTE FROM THE WRITER

The five short plays that make up *Oh, The Humanity and other good intentions* move toward feeling by way of thought, and toward gratitude by way of loss. These largely sane plays feature people alone or in pairs, or both, attempting to present themselves in the best light, or ultimately, desperately, in any light. Inadvertently vulnerable, or unconsciously callous, or both, the characters here realise that they are stuck in a body that will fail, and they try to put the best face on it. They are, at times, like all of us, unsure of who they are, what they want, and what exactly they're on the way to. Is it a funeral or a christening? Is it both or neither? Though this might all seem hazy and conditional, it might all in fact be painstaking and absolute. This is life, for the Problematical Animal.

Will Eno

CAST

Tony Bell
Lucy Ellinson
John Kirk

CREATIVE & PRODUCTION TEAM

Will Eno	Writer
Erica Whyman	Director
Andrew Stephenson	Designer
Kev Tweedy	Lighting Designer
Leif Jordansson	Composer
Michaela Kennen	Dialect Coach
Chris Slater	Production Manager
Colin Holman	Company Manager
Daniel Read	Deputy Stage Manager
Lucy Crimmens	Assistant Stage Manager / Dresser

WILL ENO Writer

Will Eno lives in Brooklyn. His most recent play, *The Realistic Joneses*, premiered at the Yale Repertory Theatre in April 2012. His play *Title and Deed* premiered at the Pershing Square Signature Center, in June 2012. His play *Thom Pain (based on nothing)*, which played at the Edinburgh Festival, the Soho Theatre in London, the DR2 in New York, and in translation around the world, was a finalist for the 2005 Pulitzer Prize for Drama. His other plays include *Tragedy: a tragedy*, *The Flu Season*, and *Middletown*. His play *Gnit*, a new adaptation of Ibsen's *Peer Gynt*, will premiere at the Actors Theatre of Louisville, in the spring of 2013.

ERICA WHYMAN Director

Erica has been Chief Executive of Northern Stage since 2005. Previously, she was Artistic Director of the Gate Theatre and before that Southwark Playhouse. At the Gate Erica championed Will Eno's work, producing the UK premiere of *Tragedy, a tragedy* in 2001 (director Paul Miller) and directing *The Flu Season* in 2003. For Northern Stage she has directed *Son of Man*; *Ruby Moon*; *Our Friends in the North*; *A Christmas Carol*; *A Doll's House*; *Look Back in Anger*; *Hansel and Gretel*; *Oh! What a Lovely War* (nominated for two TMA awards); *The Wind in the Willows*; *Who's Afraid of Virginia Woolf* (in co-production with Sheffield Theatres for which she was nominated for best director at the TMA awards); the UK premiere of *Oh, The Humanity* in September 2011, and *The Glass Slipper*. Other directing work includes: *The Birthday Party* (Sheffield Crucible); *The Shadow of a Boy* (National Theatre); *Marieluise, Witness* and *Les Justes* (Gate Theatre); *The Winter's Tale* and *The Glass Slipper* (Southwark Playhouse); *The Gambler*, *Oblomov* and 6 solo shows by Ben Moor for the Pleasance in Edinburgh.

ANDREW STEPHENSON Designer
Andrew is a freelance designer. For Northern
Stage he has designed *Truce, On Top of the
Town, Thumbelina, The Goblin Who Saved Christmas,
Tattercoats, The Prince and The Penguin* & *The
Little Boy Who Lost the Morning*. Also, *Pick & Mix
Youth Festival* (Live Theatre); *Golden Tails* (Theatre
Sans Frontiers); *Building Palaces* and *Best in the
World* (Unfolding Theatre) and *Underneath the
Floorboards* (BalletLORENT).

KEV TWEEDY Lighting Designer
Kev is Chief Electrician at Northern Stage. He has toured
internationally as a relighter and has also worked as far
afield as South Africa. Lighting design work includes *The
New Tenant, Blaze* and *Manifesto for a New City, Shhh a
Christmas Story* (Northern Stage); *Hand Me Down* (The
Empty Space); *Building Palaces* and *Best in the World*
(Unfolding Theatre).

LEIF JORDANSSON Composer
Leif is a composer, sound artist and performer who lives
in Stockholm, Sweden. He was last at Northern Stage
with the installation *n.waves* together with video artist
Peter Norrman. Recent productions include *Stockholm
East* (film by Simon Kaijser); *The Little Mermaid* (dance
theatre for the Royal Dramatic Theatre in Stockholm)
and *Grow in the Dark* (a self-playing theatre). Leif has
released a number of CDs and digital releases including
Stockholm East, De halvt dolda (Those Half Hidden);
The Comet and *The Doll Maker* on brus & knaster
and *n.waves, Miniatures* and *Inter-view* as digital
releases. In September a new documentary *Deep
Trouble in Lake Victoria* (film by Bengt Löfgren) will
open with Jordansson's music. For more information
see www.jordansson.net

MICHAELA KENNEN Dialect Coach
Theatre: *Who's Afraid of Virginia Woolf* (Northern Stage); *The History Boys, Market Boy, Caroline or Change, Thérèse Raquin, The Rose Tattoo,* (National Theatre); *Cabaret* (Lyric Theatre); *Jesus Jumped the Train* (Trafalgar Studios); *Hairspray* (Shaftsbury); *Love Never Dies* (Adelphi); *The Country Girl* (Apollo); *Pagliacci* (ENO); *Songs from a Hotel Bedroom* (ROH); *High School Musical 1 & 2* (Hammersmith Apollo/Tour); *Fame* (Tour); *The Government Inspector, The Glass Menagerie, Vernon God Little, The Brothers Size and Eurydice* (Young Vic); *Dreams of Violence* (Out of Joint); *She Loves Me, The Browning Version/South Downs* (Chichester/Harold Pinter Theatre); Artifacts, The Whisky Taster (The Bush); *One Monkey Don't Stop No Show* (Eclipse Theatre, Crucible); *Truth & Reconciliation, Love Love Love, The Witness* (Royal Court). Film: *Nine* (Dir Chris Menaul); *Cosi* (Dir Rob Marshall).

Bang in the creative heart of London, Soho Theatre is a major new writing theatre and a writers' development organisation of national significance. With a programme spanning theatre, comedy, cabaret and writers' events and home to a lively bar, Soho Theatre is one of the most vibrant venues on London's cultural scene.

Soho Theatre owns its own central London venue housing the intimate 150-seat Soho Theatre, our 90-seat Soho Upstairs and our new 1950s New York meets Berliner cabaret space, Soho Downstairs. Under the joint leadership of Soho's Artistic Director Steve Marmion and Executive Director Mark Godfrey, Soho Theatre now welcomes over 150,000 people a year.

'Soho Theatre was buzzing, and there were queues all over the building as audiences waited to go into one or other of the venue's spaces. I spend far too much time in half-empty theatres to be cross at the sight of an audience, particularly one that is so young, exuberant and clearly anticipating a good time.'
Lyn Gardner, *Guardian*

SOHO THEATRE BAR
Soho Theatre Bar is a vibrant, fun bar where artists and performers can regularly be seen pint in hand enjoying the company of friends and fans. Open from 9.30am until 1am, with free WiFi, serving breakfast, lunch and dinner, Soho Theatre Bar is the perfect place to meet, eat and drink before and after our shows.

SOHO THEATRE ONLINE
Giving you the latest information and previews of upcoming shows, Soho Theatre can be found on facebook, twitter and youtube as well as at sohotheatre.com.

HIRING THE THEATRE
An ideal venue for a variety of events, we have a range of spaces available for hire in the heart of the West End. Meetings, conferences, parties, civil ceremonies, rehearsed readings and showcases with support from our professional theatre team to assist in your events' success. For more information, please see our website sohotheatre.com/hires or to hire space at Soho Theatre, email hires@sohotheatre.com and to book an event in Soho Theatre Bar, email sohotheatrebar@sohotheatre.com.

Soho Theatre is supported by Arts Council England and Westminster City Council.

Registered Charity No: 267234

THANK YOU

We are immensely grateful to our fantastic Soho Theatre Friends and Supporters. Soho Theatre is supported by Arts Council England and Westminster City Council. This Theatre has the support of the Pearson Playwrights' Scheme sponsored by Pearson plc.

Principal Supporters
Nicholas Allott
Jimmy Carr
Jack and Linda Keenan
Amelia and Neil Mendoza
Lady Susie Sainsbury
Carolyn Ward

Corporate Sponsors
Baites Wells & Braithwaite
Cameron Mackintosh Ltd
Caprice Holdings Ltd
Dusthouse
Financial Express
Granta
The Groucho Club
Hall and Partners
Latham & Watkins LLP
Left Bank Pictures
Nexo
Oberon Books Ltd
Overbury Leisure
Ptarmigan Media
Quo Vadis
Seabright Productions Ltd
Soundcraft
SSE Audio Group

Trusts & Foundations
The Andor Charitable Trust
Austin & Hope Pilkington Trust
The Boris Karloff Charitable Foundation
Bruce Wake Charitable Trust
The Charles Rifkind and Jonathan Levy Charitable Settlement
City Bridge Trust
The David and Elaine Potter Foundation
The Earmark Trust
The 8th Earl of Sandwich Memorial Trust
Eranda Foundation
Equity Charitable Trust
The Fenton Arts Trust
The Goldsmiths' Company
The Harold Hyam Wingate Foundation
Miss Hazel M Wood Charitable Trust
Hyde Park Place Estate Charity
The John Ellerman Foundation
John Lyon's Charity
JP Getty Junior Charitable Trust
The Kobler Trust
The Mackintosh Foundation

The Mohamed S. Farsi Foundation
The Rose Foundation
The Royal Victoria Hall Foundation
The Foundation for Sport and the Arts
Sir Siegmund Warburg's Voluntary Settlement
St Giles in the Fields and William Shelton
The St James's Piccadilly Charity
Educational Charity
Teale Charitable Trust
The Thistle Trust

Soho Theatre Best Friends
Johan and Paris Christofferson
Dominic Collier
Richard Collins
Miranda Curtis
David Day
Cherry and Rob Dickins
Wendy Fisher
Sue Fletcher
Hedley and Fiona Goldberg
Norma Heyman
Isobel and Michael Holland
Beatrice Hollond
Hils Jago, Amused Moose Comedy
Lady Caroline Mactaggart
Christina Minter
Rajasana Otiende
Suzanne Pirret
Amy Ricker
Ian Ritchie and Jocelyne van den Bossche
Ann Stanton
Alex Vogel
Garry Watts
Sian and Matthew Westerman
Hilary and Stuart Williams

Soho Theatre Dear Friends
Natalie Bakova
Quentin Bargate
Norman Bragg
Neil and Sarah Brener
Roddy Campbell
Caroline and Colin Church
Giles Fernando
Jonathan Glanz
Geri Haliwell
Anya Hindmarch and James Seymour

Shappi Khorsandi
Lynne Kirwin
Michael Kunz
James and Margaret Lancaster
Anita and Brook Land
Nick Mason
Annette Lynton Mason
Andrew and Jane McManus
Roger and Bridget Myddelton
Karim Nabih
Sir Tim Rice
Sue Robertson
Nigel Wells
Andrea Wong
Matt Woodford
Christopher Yu

Soho Theatre Good Friends
Jonathan and Amanda Baines
Mike Baxter
Valerie Blin
Jon Briggs
David Brooks
Mathew Burkitt
Victoria Carr
Chris Carter
Jeremy Conway
Sharon Eva Degen
Geoffrey and Janet Eagland
Gail & Michael Flesch
Daniel and Joanna Friel
Stephen Garrett, Kudos Films
Alban Gordon
Marianna Gorenstein
Doug Hawkins
Thomas Hawtin
Etan Ilfeld
Jennifer Jacobs
David King
Lorna Klimt
David and Linda Lakhdhir
Amanda Mason
Ryan Miller
Catherine Nendick
Martin Ogden
Alan Pardoe
Andrew Perkins
Andrew Powell
Geraint Rogers
Barry Serjent
Nigel Silby
Lesley Symons
Dr Sean White
Liz Young

We would also like to thank those supporters who wish to stay anonymous as well as all of our Soho Theatre Friends.

Supported using public funding by
ARTS COUNCIL ENGLAND
LOTTERY FUNDED

Supported by
City of Westminster

NORTHERN
STAGE

Northern Stage is the North East of England's largest producing theatre, with three flexible stages and a diverse programme both of performances and opportunities to make and discover theatre. We make ambitious, intelligent, enjoyable theatre for adults, children and across generations. We have a reputation for reviving modern classic plays in fresh adaptations for national tours (most recently *Close The Coalhouse Door* directed by Samuel West and co-produced with Live theatre) as well as for creating bold new work. Alongside our own productions Northern Stage has extensive partnership with the best UK theatre-makers including Kneehigh, Gecko, ETT, Headlong, Cheek By Jowl, Tim Crouch, Unlimited Theatre, Third Angel and Slunglow, ensuring their work is seen in the North East. We regularly collaborate with international theatre-makers (in 2007 we co-produced *Lipsynch* with Robert Lepage) and we have been a partner in the World Shakespeare Festival.

Our extensive Creative Residencies programme supports local and national theatre-makers to develop their work at Northern Stage, including Title Pending, our annual award for new theatre (recent winners include Greyscale, Kirsty Housley and The Paper Birds). We run a year-round programme of projects and events encouraging people of all ages and backgrounds to take part in making theatre.

In August 2012, for the first time, we will be running a venue at the Edinburgh Fringe Festival. Northern Stage at St Stephen's will provide a high-profile platform for the work of artists making work in the North of England. We want to shout about and showcase some of the innovative and exciting work that is being created in this part of the world.

Newcastle
City Council

Supported using public funding by
ARTS COUNCIL
ENGLAND

NORTHERN STAGE STAFF

Rob Brown	**Head of Sound/AV**
Sarah Brown	**PA to Production Manager and CEO**
Mark Calvert	**Creative Associate**
Amy Carter	**Participation Coordinator**
Susan Coffer	**Administrative Director**
Jamie Corbett	**Data and Sales Analyst**
Jo Cundall	**Programming Manager**
John Disley	**Front of House Manager**
Anthony Easter	**Technician (Stage)**
Frances Easter	**Theatre Manager**
Amy Fawdington	**Communications Manager**
Richard Flood	**Deputy Head of Sound/AV**
Peter Flynn	**Director of Communications and Sales**
Brenda Gray	**Executive Assistant**
Louise Gregory	**Deputy Chief (LX)**
Jane Hall	**Development Manager**
Colin Holman	**Company Manager**
Kelly Jackson	**Communications Officer**
Ruth Johnson	**Participation Manager**
Kylie Lloyd	**Director of Participation**
Ruth McClure	**Sales and Box Office Manager**
Darren McGowan	**Deputy Head of Workshop**
Joanne McKenna	**Director of Finance**
Susan Mulholland	**Deputy Director of Participation**
Edmund Nickols	**Director of Operations**
Nina Ritson	**Development Assistant**
Andrew Sharp	**Technician (Stage)**
Jill Sharp	**Finance Officer**
Chris Slater	**Production Manager**
Casey Spence	**Digital Co-ordinator**
Alison Stringer	**Wardrobe Supervisor**
Adham Tawfik	**Deputy Front of House Manager**
Kevin Tweedy	**Chief Electrician**
Erica Whyman	**Chief Executive**
Graham Wilson	**Technician (LX)**
Mike Wymark	**Head of Workshops**

Board Members
Fiona Standfield (Chair), Tim Bailey, Jonathan Brown, Lynn Charlton, Professor Eric Cross, Jo Darby, Andy Hudson, Malcolm Page, Keith Proudfoot, Donna Swan, Paul Taylor, Linda Tuttiett and Jean-Pierre van Zyl

The text went to press before the end of rehearsals
and so may differ slightly from the play as performed.

OH, THE HUMANITY
and other good intentions

Will Eno

OH, THE HUMANITY
and other good intentions

BEHOLD THE COACH, IN A BLAZER, UNINSURED

LADIES AND GENTLEMEN, THE RAIN

ENTER THE SPOKESWOMAN, GENTLY

THE BULLY COMPOSITION

OH, THE HUMANITY

OBERON BOOKS
LONDON

WWW.OBERONBOOKS.COM

First published in 2008 by Oberon Books Ltd
521 Caledonian Road, London N7 9RH
Tel: +44 (0) 20 7607 3637 / Fax: +44 (0) 20 7607 3629
e-mail: info@oberonbooks.com
www.oberonbooks.com

Reprinted in 2011 (twice), 2012

"Behold the Coach, in a Blazer, Uninsured" appeared in a slightly different version under the title "Behold the Coach, in Sorrow, Uninsured" in *Harper's Magazine* (February 2003).

A catalogue record for this book is available from the British Library.

PB ISBN: 978-1-84002-832-4
E ISBN: 978-1-84943-628-1

Cover design by Michael Windsor-Ungureanu

Printed, bound and converted
by CPI Group (UK) Ltd, Croydon, CR0 4YY.

Visit www.oberonbooks.com to read more about all our books and to buy them. You will also find features, author interviews and news of any author events, and you can sign up for e-newsletters so that you're always first to hear about our new releases.

Contents

Oh, the Humanity and other good intentions was first produced at the Flea Theater, New York, on 3 November 2007, with the following cast:

Marisa Tomei
Brian Hutchison
Drew Hildebrand

Directed by Jim Simpson
Sets by Kyle Chepulis
Lighting by Brian Aldous
Costumes by Claudia Brown
Sound by Jill B C DuBoff
Video/projection by Dustin O'Neill

First produced in the UK, by special arrangement with SUBIAS, at Northern Stage, Newcastle upon Tyne, on 9 September 2011 with the following cast:

Tony Bell
Lucy Ellinson
John Kirk

Directed by Erica Whyman
Designed by Andrew Stephenson
Lighting Design by Kevin Tweedy
Composition by Leif Jordansson
Sound Design by Rob Brown
Dialect Coach Michaela Kennen

The author, who is mainly American, and who might not be an author but for the following, would like to thank the following, who are mainly English: Jack Bradley, Chris Campbell, Daisy Heath, Gordon Lish, Paul Miller, Joe Sola, Kester Thompson, and Erica Whyman.

BEHOLD THE COACH, IN A BLAZER, UNINSURED

Dramatis Persona

THE COACH

Setting

A press conference. A table with a paper cup and several microphones on it.

BEHOLD THE COACH, IN A BLAZER, UNINSURED

THE COACH

He enters, places his keys, cigarettes, etc, on the table. Sits down.

All right, everybody, let's just get going. You people know what I've come here to probably say. This should all come as all as no surprise. The phrase, of course, you are familiar with. It was a "building year," this last year was. We suffered some losses, yes, we suffered some, last season, and we had to start out all over, in a fashion; we had to come at this thing as if it were a—you folks in the press can tell me if this is a pleonasm—a new beginning. We made some changes here and there and here and we made these, mainly, mostly, with the fans in mind, because we wanted the fans to be happy, in our minds we wanted the fans to love us. And I think they should be happy, in my mind I think they should love us.

Listen, last year was not the easiest year. The plan was that it would be for building, for rebuilding, for replacing what was lost, replenishing what was gone, and trying to reverse a routine of losing that had grown in-grown and somehow strangely proud. Our strategy was, in theory, to betray that which had become merely habit, to betray our very fear, the very thing that's kept us alive, the thing that says to us: Don't cross the street without looking both ways first; Don't speak your mind and certainly never your heart.

Brief pause.

But habit's a hard habit to break.

Brief pause.

And was it only habit that kept us from dropping to our knees in the middle of the street and sobbing and begging "Can somebody help me, please?" Was it just mere routine that kept us on our feet, with our mouths shut and our hands in our pockets?

One night, after practice—some of you might appreciate this—I found myself standing in the unforgivable light of a grocery store, staring at my reflection in a freezer, and realizing: "You're not having a bad day—this is just what you look like, now. This is who the years are making you." The praying kind probably would have prayed. I just wanted to grab a courtesy phone and beg into it: "Could someone come to the front of the store and clean up the spill that is my life on this earth? Could somebody please just somehow help me through this punishing crushing nauseating sorrow?"

Brief pause.

So that's what this last year was. We had to look hard at a few things and, surprise surprise, we found that they looked hard back. But in many ways, I think we have to be happy. We sold some hot dogs. We got some sun, some fresh air. We played some close games—some of them, even, we were still in until right up to the end. It was the life, it really was, and, granted, yeah, no, this was not the greatest year. Some people are saying it was barely even a shambles. I'm sure there's a more charitable view, but, okay: fair enough. Fair enough.

Brief pause.

I had no idea how hard hard was until this year came around. Nights, whole nights, weeks of nights, in a row. I bet I walked a thousand miles up and down my street alone. I came home and went out, walking. My eyes all runny, just walking, counting up the things I don't have anymore, thinking of the Fair Lady of my own incompetent sonnets. Who I lost, by the way. Or, failed to win. Or, forfeited, in some miserable show of inwardness, or downwardness, or shame.

Brief pause.

It was a hard year. Tough schedule.

Brief pause.

> My love is like a sunset, stunning, and then over.
> And in the year since her, there has not been
> A single thing but ashes and formalities.
> A year of cigarette butts and minor car crashes.
> Rosemary, for remembrance;
> Glucosamine and Chondroitin, for the joints.
> And I will never love
> any thing or body again.
> And I am not young and handsome.
> And I could not coach a gallon of water
> Out of a paper bag.

Pause.

So. That was some poetry. And, so, yes, obviously, I've had my doubts. I've had what you people might call Personal Problems. But I tried. To run things different. With a little elegance, a new uniform. I tried writing that thing about the sunset. I tried to act with some sense of honor and calm amidst the urgency and vulgarity of the—I don't know. You tell me, you lived through it, too, you lived right straight through it, too. What was this year? Can we even—I don't know. Christ Jesus Christ.

He directs the question toward a person in the audience.

What did you feel, this past year? Of what would you be speaking, if you were sitting here, this year, speaking of the last? And did any one of us have what he would call a winning season? And what would that even look like? And could someone tell me, while we're at it, when is High School over, when comes High School to its high-schoolish end? When begins my true life as me on Earth? Because I really don't understand when the seriousness is supposed to start. And I'm so filled with wanting, I so crave to know, just a little anything, a fact, a meaning, a song, even a jingle. A little lullaby, to be put to sleep by, to sleep. I'd like to know a real poem. By someone other than me, with a vocabulary other than mine. Just a gentle little rhymey poem for the old boy with the clipboard and whistle.

Pause.

It was a real hell of a hell of a time, this year. What's that saying? About the penguin? And the fifty-yard dash? Well, that's exactly what it was. Really.

Brief pause.

It was a trying time. A building year. An endless gorgeous gorgeous endless loss. Which now is now over. And we have how many more left left to us to lose?

Pause.

Now, I know you guys in the press are going to have a field day with some of the things I've said up here today.

He stands.

And I know you're probably thinking: Something seems to have kind of snuffed out the fire this guy had when we hired him. You're probably thinking: Could someone in this condition ever get it all together and grab it with both hands and win us a championship, given the fact that he's halfway-gone in distraction and mourning for a woman who was solely herself in every inch of her body and might have been the best thing that ever happened to him, assuming he's even capable of letting someone happen to him? Could someone like this ever show us how not to lose? Well, I'll tell you, because I came here to tell you a few things. I came here to feel the burn from your flash bulbs, and to speak a few things into that harsh light, my heart included. And the answer is, I don't know. I don't know if I can lead anyone to victory, or even lead anyone anywhere. I don't know if my plan is a good one, or even if I have one.

I am asking you to just let me be still. To let me turn my face upward to the heavens, while the rest of me slumps earthward, and let me say, you've got to please just hear me and let me stand here and say, to the sky, or the ceiling, and to all of you, and I quote:

Brief pause.

I don't know. In general. And, in particular, in particular.

All I know is that someone has to be everywhere. And I—it's hard not to realize—I am the one who is up here, now. Before all of you who are sitting there, there. I am the one in the position I'm in. I sit before you, as that man. In spite of all the grim realities and lonely terms of this great game and all that we who play it face. And I lived as that man through this last year, past. And I think I should be happy. I do. I think we should all be very terribly proud and happy, and happy and afraid, and afraid and thrilled, really thrilled to death at the upcoming year and all of the life it will naturally contain.

This is my feeling on this.

We probably only have time for one question.

Blackout.

END

LADIES AND GENTLEMEN, THE RAIN

Dramatis Personae

GENTLEMAN

LADY

Setting

Each of the characters is recording a videotape, for the purpose of employing a dating service.

General notes concerning staging

Each of the characters is seated on a stool, the LADY at stage left, the GENTLEMAN at stage right. Two cameras are set on tripods before them (these can also simply be implied). Though there is no physical barrier between them, the two never regard one another, and never acknowledge the presence of the other's body on stage. At certain times, they stand, preen, move forward or walk around to behind their chairs, for the point of emphasis.

LADIES AND GENTLEMEN, THE RAIN

GENTLEMAN and LADY, in low light, are seated as described above. The two are straightening a collar, smoothing a dress, generally preparing to be videotaped. Lights up.

LADY

Is it started? Are we started? I'll wait.

GENTLEMAN

Hi. I'm a little nervous. Who isn't? Anyway. Where to begin. I guess there's no need for me to try describing myself, since, well, here I am, here. I look like this. I don't know whether that's good news. But, okay, what else? I'm good at grocery shopping. Fairly good. I shine my own shoes. I don't try to say anything funny when someone close has died. I don't stop drinking. I know women have their times. I'm average-sized. Of average intelligence. Blood pressure, too, I guess.

LADY

Sorry—now? Sorry.

GENTLEMAN

No pets, but, I have a great love and understanding of the dog. Although almost none of any other animal. For instance, once some geese came flying over me and I thought, "Now where the hell are they going?" Another time, a moth was bothering me by flying at my lamp. So I turned it off. A third animal incident concerns a mourning dove, and how quick I was to make it wish that we had never met.

He pauses.

I'm hardly ever like that.

LADY

Looking into the light.

I can't tell if there's anyone… I guess I'll just start talking. I love the outdoors. Air and weather, the sky. I'm the type to like walking around, with the little book, trying to identify trees or plants. I like it indoors, too, don't get me wrong, The Great Indoors. But I love being outside. I like swimming. I have five bathing suits. No, four, because one time I was—no, I was right, it's five. It's not important.

Brief pause.

I never saw myself doing this. I've seen myself doing things, strangely. But not this.

Brief pause.

Anyway. Feelings, me, thoughts. I'm always surprised when the ocean gets really quiet. And I don't get why breaking the sound barrier should make so much noise. Things like that. Everything seems too quiet or too loud. I'm torn exactly in half, about fifty per cent of the time. This is most days. Although, other times, things aren't quite so clear. For instance, once, I couldn't get over it, but there it was, and you go figure it out.

GENTLEMAN

I have different interests. I enjoy not traveling. I don't speak any second language. Fine dining, live music, and cinema can come and go. I stay out of museums. I stay away from home. I don't have a favorite food, but I guess I like cholesterol. I tend not to speak unless spoken to. In the summer, I like not having the heat on. In the winter, I like to not sit in front of a fan. I try to look on the bright side. I am not, as I look around myself, currently bleeding.

LADY

I'm one of those people who believes there are two kinds of people. And these can be divided into billions of other kinds of people, which time prohibits me from, you know, I don't know… But I have my type. My types, I guess. I like watching people clapping for something they really like, and, watching someone sign his signature. I'm also attracted to men who black out when asked a difficult question. (*A small quick smile.*) I guess I mean I like it when I feel I'm really being heard.

GENTLEMAN

When I was little, I…wait. God. Weird. I forget what I was going to say. "When I was little." It's completely gone.

LADY

Dislikes? Rudeness. Untimely remarks. Bossy…bossiness. Ostentation. Also, nerve damage and heart disease. Heat stroke, also. Heat death. Regular people death. The dying of U.S. presidents. The death of a family dog. Alice, for instance. The passing of eras, decades, everything, all this time going by, getting old, dying, in a sense. Like grass. Like annual flowers. Like something, like that. Like people.

She pauses.

None of that really puts me in the mood. But I guess there's a chance that any of it could.

GENTLEMAN

While LADY has been speaking, he has been trying to remember the thing he forgot. He decides to move on, shakes his head, almost imperceptibly.

Anyway. Onward. I am such a fan of shoulder-length hair. And any color eyes. And I like how women talk. I have faults, obviously. Some weak points are my knees and back. And I don't have any patience for things that take a long time. Although, it should be said, I'm usually very deeply just waiting. Bugs fly in my mouth sometimes, because I'm just standing there, full of want, full of open-mouthed wonder. I stay like that long enough to give them time to fly out, because, although unknowing, I am not unkind.

Brief pause.

I like walking. I'll run, if I have to. Or stay still. But you're never going to find me shaking on the floor, biting into my own hand, and crying out into the daylight. Except, sometimes. But really only rarely, on those occasions.

LADY

Give life a go with this attractive and elegant woman. This sensitive and sympathetic, maybe somewhat removed, I don't know, somewhat ingoing, but, sensitive, sympathetic...

GENTLEMAN

See the world. See the—I don't know—world. See some sort of...

LADY

You know what,—

GENTLEMAN

Did you ever feel—

LADY

I don't know. God. Sometimes,…

GENTLEMAN

Sometimes, I just want to do someone over and have that be it. Sometimes, I—quote—love, with nothing but my hands and the dried-out words I've practiced and remembered. Quote love.

LADY

A lot of times, it's only to somehow make someone pay for my former life as a child. A lot of times I don't feel anything but the come on my stomach.

GENTLEMAN

"I'm not what I look like," I want to say to people who think I look like a certain kind of person. Even though, when I think about it, I see how I could be wrong.

LADY

I'm sorry. Sometimes I feel differently. Sometimes, I find the world so, I don't know, so attractive, and I look at it, the world, and I think of all the different parts of it, all the people and things that can happen, and I think, Wow. Ouch. But mainly, Wow.

GENTLEMAN

I take it back. Forget what I just said.

LADY

What else is a person supposed to say?

GENTLEMAN

Who doesn't have a few bad days, out of the twenty-five thousand? The twenty thousand?

LADY

She glances at a piece of paper, obviously something she's prepared in advance:

"Hear the call of the evening, of the night, of a lone person, the call of a trembling paragraph of speech, of my favorite language, English."

Brief pause.

It was my minor.

GENTLEMAN

This is from a thing that I, I don't know...

He reads:

"Let's go out, into the night, into rancor, over shiny highways, down grand canyons and tree-lined dead-ends, milady and I, into and unto the rude world awaiting." It's from this letter I tried writing.

LADY

I want to start a family. Or, at least, finish one. Either way, that would be later. What else can I tell you? "You."

Brief pause.

I like wine. Summer. Same as anyone. I wear dresses. I used to know how much I weighed, soaking wet. You know that old phrase. I used to... My first...

Pause.

I have this picture. In my mind. In it, I'm soaking wet. From running and sweating and the rain or from the feeling I'm having. Everything is all—I'm sorry… I've lived with it for as long as I've lived with anything. I can see the sky. I can see the trees, bending, and the birds, flying away somewhere. And me. And I'm running, in a dress, and it's raining. There's the feeling of someone else, of some ghostly You, there or just about to be there. I'm always running. Not away from or toward, just running. And the sky keeps changing, and me underneath it. Gray, blue, white, dark gray, dark gray. I'm in a meadow, usually, near some woods, looking at everything, at all the natural forces and the leaves moving, trying to find some secret order in it, some higher darker good. Some lasting helpful truth other than that the world moves on, destroying things. Me, for example—for example, myself.

GENTLEMAN

As for yourself, you're of a sunny disposition. You have what shampoo bottles would describe as normal hair. You like seeing those plywood signs that say "Pick your own berries." Sometimes you like to cook and clean. Sometimes you don't. You're quiet in bed, unless in the middle of some great woe or, I don't know, something.

Brief pause.

Sometimes, you wish you were dead, but you'll probably die wishing you could live, and you know that. You imagine things a certain way. You draw little drawings of things. You were young. You get scared to death. You start shaking. I know you're out there, somewhere. Shaking.

LADY

You're always in the distance. Athletic, lean—or I don't know. Just *describable*, somehow. Recognizable. To me. People can see your life story in your posture, in the way you look at things and hold yourself. You probably collect something. You were once suicidal, but have since lost interest. You're looking for me. Someone like me. I've been described as The Girl Next Door, by neighbors. I'm occasionally given to crying in the daytime. I'm given to wearing no shoes. I'm given to suffering from cervical cancer, disorder in the nervous system, immense pain in my lower back, and fits of unspeakable but finally ultimately not-uncommon anguish in the night. I'm given to probably almost everything, eventually. I like horseback riding.

GENTLEMAN

I like riding horses. One time I fell. I did something to my shoulder. It healed. But I got older and older. And that kept happening. And all that time, I kept having this, I don't know—I'm not the type to have visions—but, this vision. I'm standing in your yard. In the country. I don't know how I got here. It's fall. The weather is always cold and rainy, unpromising, good. You're coming home, holding groceries, fooling with your keys, looking up. It's so simple. Notice me. Please care that I'm standing on your property, in the rain. Acknowledge my soaked clothes somehow. I want to say something, just call over to you. I just want to say, Hey, hi, it's me. After all these years.

Brief pause.

This isn't imaginary. I know it isn't. I'm looking at you and asking you, I'm not alone, right now, on Earth, right now, am I?

He whispers.

Fuck.

LADY

Isn't a life just a history of the times when you did or didn't turn? This is how I always saw it. This. With you right there, but not yet, and the clouds all dramatic. I just want you to turn. Please come toward me. Just look at me for once in my life. I'm saying Please. I'm saying Look.

GENTLEMAN

I know what happens in life. But I don't know if I'll be alone when it does. It seems like a big thing not to know.

LADY

The birds and animals and everything are all quiet.

GENTLEMAN

I picture us in a cemetery.

LADY

What a beautiful day.

GENTLEMAN

Standing under a tree. Arms touching. Our arms touching.

LADY

Just the rain dripping on the leaves. Like in every poem ever written. Just you and me, side by side.

GENTLEMAN

I just want to be calm. And to be able to look without having to look away.

LADY

I want to feel home for once. Together with someone in the regular world but also together in another little world of our own devisement. I believe in this. My picture of life. Why would I keep having it? I read the newspapers but I still believe in this.

GENTLEMAN

I feel weak. I'm worried I'm weak. I get nervous, sometimes. I don't know what to say, sometimes. Which is weak.

LADY

I've waited and waited, and, look at me, I still am. In all recorded time, what were they recording, if not the secret and sideways dreams of people like us, lone people in serious wait. Like it's what we're born for.

Brief pause.

Devisement's a word, isn't it?

GENTLEMAN

When I used to be younger, it was my belief that you met some other person. I believed that the world was small. I thought that the world was my mother and father. And then you find someone, some other person, and you just go, simple as that, you just go off somewhere, and get old slowly somewhere, in love. I believed that people were perfect. And life went on forever.

He pauses.

I was right. About everything.

LADY

I enjoy tennis.

GENTLEMAN

Please send a photograph.

LADY

A sense of humor is important.

GENTLEMAN

You could send a drawing.

LADY

I would walk all over the bleeding world—

GENTLEMAN

I'd like to see your handwriting.

LADY

—I would, for a man who would tell me the time.

GENTLEMAN

I swear I'll answer.

LADY

I'm the type of girl who likes music. And who, on Earth, is *not* the type of girl who likes music. I'm looking for someone to talk with. I'd give up my body in this world for a single conversation.

GENTLEMAN

I'm looking for someone, and I hope that I'll know her when I see her. I am looking for something that seems so far to have been happy to have kept itself hidden.

LADY

Have I said what my name was?

GENTLEMAN

Is there a little light that's supposed to come on?

Lights fade.

END

ENTER THE SPOKESWOMAN, GENTLY

Dramatis Persona

SPOKESWOMAN FOR COUNTRY AIR

Setting

A press conference. She stands before a podium. Mounted on it are several microphones, the Country Air logo.

ENTER THE SPOKESWOMAN, GENTLY

SPOKESWOMAN

She enters.

Hello. First of all, let me just say that we are suffering with you families. Let me say, just, that we're suffering, we're staring at each other and up into the sky, like you, and that we have, while staring, tried to act. In a first very small step, we have as of tonight called off tomorrow's company picnic. I know that doesn't sound serious. We are canceling other events as well, because of the failure of the airplane. We don't know what we should do, honestly, or what we should say after doing it. But we do know the last thing anyone wants to see is us enjoying life, drinking too much and driving home drunk with someone from personnel, with a temporary tattoo and a sunburn. So, the picnic, of course, is off.

I have a father who died, incidentally. He taught me sports and going outside, picnic things. So I was just thinking about him. My father's gone, possibly as yours is, though mine died in a chair. He died sitting quietly, and not in a plane in flames, screaming downward at the speed of sound. His final resting place was an unraveling easy-chair in the living room. He was only human, and though it could have been, this was not listed as the cause of death. Countless nights beneath relatively fatherly men did nothing to lift the weight of that sad time. Excuse me, I'm sorry.

Brief pause.

I don't know what it would be good for you to do. Try those things we all try.

A pause.

As for why, it is, as of tonight, undetermined. Who knows? Weather, an act of God or some handsome pilot's drunken error? Whatever it was, here we are. And we'll try to move forward, with time, taking hard comfort in the fact that, with or without us, time is moving forward, too.

A pause.

But, so, yes—it was flight 514, the night flight to Johnston, and there were, at this time, no survivors. We have been told so little so far. Gravity, we trust, was a factor. Did they know when it was still up that it was coming down? We hope not. We hope they felt secure on their airplane, as do we on our earth, and denied the fact of their coming doom, as do we ours. We hope they were enjoying the in-flight movie. Which was a Finnish film called *The Bleeding Parade.* I don't know if these small details are helpful.

I do have some news, or, business, some awful business. Families of the deceased get a round-trip ticket, as well as a bereavement allowance, which should help with travel and funeral plans. You get so little, sometimes. You people whose loved one is gone, you people who are, in fact, in fact, also going, dying, but from the inside out, from having time go by, as died my dad, as will probably die me, not from doing anything daring, not flying, or skydiving, just sitting there being human with your mouths open, looking so sweet and deaf. What a world, isn't it. All of us. There may be other compensation.

I want to say—I'm the spokesperson, it's my job, and it's not easy—but I want to say to you: I understand, I think I understand. You waited and waited at the airport, you raced there in the first place, through unspeakable traffic, and the parking situation, and then you got to the proper gate and waited and they didn't come and didn't come and the monitor said DELAYED and I'm sure it was confusing, and then frustrating, and now just so sad. And can these things, can any sad things, ever even be compared? Is it insulting to you if I think they can? I'm sorry. My degree was in Hospitality Management. I fell into this job through an acquaintance in the field.

A brief pause.

We're all going there, wherever, at different speeds, in different styles. I guess I am, as the spokesperson here, speaking to you, asking you to look around. Look at your hands. They used to be so tiny. Now they're not, and they're old. There are lines in our faces around our eyes from years of just laughing and using the wrong soap. The body is its own disaster area. The human face is a call for help. *Help, We need help, We are in flames, Port engine out, No radio. Landing gear is mangled, Radar is blank, Please foam the runway, We are coming in, coming home and down, and so shall you all.*

A pause.

I'm sorry. We don't have a formalized tack we take in events like this. We understand how little there is to say, but that something must be said. We are grateful that nights like this are rare, that Country Air has a record of somewhat excellence—but I know that doesn't help. I want to help, but I know I can't, and I know that doesn't help. So, help me, and hear me, and understand, I beg you, that I'm just saying... Maybe it was quiet. Maybe all the lights and engines were out and it was just a dark and quiet thing falling through the night. The whole thing coming apart like a comet, but, also, unlike anything. And maybe, I'm just saying, maybe it was the high point of something, maybe it was somehow something's perfect ending. Maybe all the people in the crashing plane were thinking of you, the soon-to-be still-living, were wishing you were there, assuming useless crash positions among the blankets and little liquor bottles, living, busy, falling through the air, a silence in the silence, about to make a serious noise. Maybe they felt famous. Or special or chosen. Loved, maybe, somehow, finally. I don't know. We don't.

A pause.

This was, by the way, an experienced experienced crew. They had flown several thousands of hours. They knew what they were doing.

A pause.

We're so sorry. We wish it could have been another way, but it wasn't. We are asking you to be grateful. Here we are, that's all, just us, here, still, and we want you to see the miracle of this. Officially, we would like you to feel giddy, for your heart to pound, for you to feel blessed, that the plane stayed up for as long as it did. That the plane could even fly at all. That the thing actually got off the ground in the first place.

This is all I can currently say.

I'm so sorry.

I would tell you more if I knew more.

Lights down.

END

THE BULLY COMPOSITION

Dramatis Personae

PHOTOGRAPHER
male, 30-50

ASSISTANT
female, 30-40

(In the program, no roles should be listed. Only the actors' names should appear, e.g., "John Smith. Jane Jones." The reason for this is to encourage the audience to more easily accept the possibility that this is an improvisation.)

Setting

Theatre.

Stage Properties

A camera (with a flash), a tripod, a light meter, some lights. A folder full of photos and papers.

THE BULLY COMPOSITION

PHOTOGRAPHER and ASSISTANT enter. PHOTOGRAPHER begins to set up a camera (with a flash, perhaps some remote flash devices) and tripod, aimed at the audience. ASSISTANT has a folder filled with papers, photographs, etc. ASSISTANT looks around at the theatre and audience, checking light meter readings. Both PHOTOGRAPHER and ASSISTANT speak mainly to the audience, and do so in a very natural way that must seem extemporaneous, but in a way that should also, at times, express just as naturally an intense gravity.

ASSISTANT

Don't be nervous. Just act natural.

PHOTOGRAPHER

Fidgeting with camera.

This should only take a minute.

Brief pause.

To make a record of your souls.

ASSISTANT

Don't blink.

Looking around at the light in the theater, checking a meter reading.

We may need more light. I don't know, maybe not.

Brief pause. Pulling a small antique photograph, wrapped in a protective cover, out of a folder. The photograph, though the audience won't really be able to see it, should be of a grotesquely mutilated corpse.

Anyway, why don't we start.

PHOTOGRAPHER

Good.

Looks through the viewfinder, sees that lens cap is still on camera, removes it.

Much better.

ASSISTANT

What we're going to be doing in this one is re-enacting, or re-creating—celebrating, too, really—a little-known photograph by an unknown photographer, depicting—well, you'll see. The title—though it's hard to make out the writing on the back—the title is "The Bully Composition." It was taken in 1898 in Cuba during the Spanish-American War. "The Splendid Little War." I'll pass this around, and, when you look at it, you can see how strangely the people

She looks at it for the first time and realizes she has the wrong photo. This is treated as only a minor inconvenience.

—and, oops, wrong one. Sorry. I have it here. Hang on one sec.

She begins looking through the papers in her folder, just as she is saying "..., wrong one."

Sorry.

She continues looking.

PHOTOGRAPHER

We'll wait.

Brief pause. He looks through the viewfinder.

"People in a Building, Seated, Breathing." That's what I'd title this. Or "Number Nineteen."

He looks again. Referring to people in seats the lens might not be able to include:

I don't know if we'll get everyone.

Brief pause.

We're all here in spirit.

During the above, ASSISTANT has begun looking in another folder.

PHOTOGRAPHER

He takes a quick look at the incorrect photograph that ASSISTANT was about to pass around. To ASSISTANT.

Maybe I could do my...

ASSISTANT, as she continues to look for the photograph, nods a quick "yes."

To audience:

So, I do a little thing, sort of a—I don't know, you'll see. It seems to be helpful, picture-taking-wise. It helps people get into a kind of—well, I hope it does, anyway—but just, the right place. It's probably weird, but, maybe it'll be good. So...

PHOTOGRAPHER begins a concerted effort at going into some kind of a trance. Pause.

Private…

Very long pause. ASSISTANT looks, occasionally and very discretely, for the photo. PHOTOGRAPHER doesn't go into a trance.

Sorry. Usually I can do it.

ASSISTANT

And, I don't think we have our photo. We're all right. Um, maybe it'd be good if we could…sorry, one second.

She whispers something to PHOTOGRAPHER. Very short exchange, between them, as they decide to move on.

To audience:

Okay. We're fine.

Very quick last peek into the folder.

We can live without it.

With little lingering anxiety, she moves gently and respectfully into the details of the photograph.

What you would see, if you could see it, is a group of American troops sitting on the ground and on boxes, staring at the camera. We are on San Juan Hill, in the Spanish-American War, July 1st. It was the single worst day of fighting, they say, the bloodiest. "The Bully Composition." Photographer unknown. The people in it have this sort of historic look in their eyes.

PHOTOGRAPHER

Almost like they were born to be in a photograph. Except, they don't really have any expressions. They're just regular people, staring straight ahead. As they—I don't know—as they try to gather the strength their post-photograph lives are going to ask of them.

ASSISTANT

Brief pause.

I think they have expressions. People always have expressions. You just have to look.

Brief pause.

What else? It's black-and-white, of course. They're right there. The people. One of them looks like he wants to cry but doesn't know what crying is. Or like it's a burden for him to have a face.

Brief pause.

There's some discrepancy about the time of day.

PHOTOGRAPHER

Somewhat dismissively.

But it's fairly clear.

ASSISTANT

Well, but there are questions.

PHOTOGRAPHER

Conceding the point, somewhat.

Yes, there are questions. You can't tell from the sky if it's morning or evening. It can look like both.

ASSISTANT

Of course, the sky. But it's not just the sky. It's the meaning of the sky. The meaning of morning or evening. Were they afraid of dying, or, happy to be alive? Did they just do something awful, or were they about to do something brave? One has his legs crossed. He's holding an apple. It's such a simple picture. You'd think we'd be able to tell.

PHOTOGRAPHER

Well, the resolution isn't great. The sky looks almost like it's done in watercolor. And the flag in the background is all blurry. And, I think—I forget—I think it's torn.

ASSISTANT

A little frayed, at the end. But, yes, blurry.

PHOTOGRAPHER

The rest is very still, sharp, the people. They had to sit like that for a while, because of the old cameras. Imagine. Nobody moving. It's very quiet. Storm clouds and maybe something else are gathering. A mosquito—and this was in the days of yellow fever and malaria—a mosquito lands on your cheek and just sits there. All quiet. You wait for the click. This was the moment.

ASSISTANT

Yes, but, possibly not—which is the interesting thing. That there can be such precision regarding the actual moment, but, so much confusion regarding the context. Or, regarding the two moments on either side.

PHOTOGRAPHER

I think it's morning.

ASSISTANT

It may be, but, I guess... I don't know. If you could see it, really look into the picture of these people's eyes—I wish I had it—I think you'd see a bigger mystery other than just what time it was. Wouldn't you? Had they just come through it all? All the shattered bones and real blood and bleeding horses and noise. Or was it still just farm boys' quiet dreams of glory, something later, something fine and right, that they were about to do? Which version were they? And what's either one supposed to look like? You'd see it, I think. The confusion, the whole trouble. It'd be there in their faces, somehow, whenever it was. Imagine that: a day, a serious day, or a night, in someone else's life. Cuts and scratches, actual dirty socks; serious doubts and homesickness. Someone else's. A splinter, an unheld hand. A war. Feel *that.* Look at a picture and feel *that.*

Brief pause.

We should try and learn to look at each other harder.

Brief pause.

If we did, well, then, maybe, then, we'd all... I don't know.

PHOTOGRAPHER

Maybe.

Pause. Gently:

Why don't we try to take this.

ASSISTANT

Take what?

PHOTOGRAPHER

This.

ASSISTANT

But, this *what?* That's what I'm trying to say.

PHOTOGRAPHER

This photograph. Is what I'm trying to say.

ASSISTANT is standing somewhere in the camera's frame. Motioning her to the side.

Could you...

She moves.

And, could you move that light down?

ASSISTANT

It's easy to feel sorry for people in a photograph, to think you understand.

Adjusting the angle of a light.

It's easy to look at a picture, wince, keep looking, and say you can't look anymore.

Referring to the light.

Like that?

PHOTOGRAPHER

PHOTOGRAPHER stares into the light, a little distracted.

Yes.

Pause.

Yeah. Good.

Referring to the extra light:

We might not even need this. It's always a compromise, with light, as to whether you…

*He continues to stare mainly into the light, throughout.
Perhaps speaks in a heightened sort of monotone.*

Private Edward Thomas; Sterling, Indiana. We're halfway up a hill that goes down the other side. Under sickening violent fire. Such insane rage over there. And over here. Mullen lost his eye and he's crying out of the other one. Foley's holding his insides. His intestines look like animals. Somebody lost a hand and it's lying in the dirt in the sun like a drawing. They told us not to shoot or move or make noise. So we're not. Americans hiding on the side of a hill, frozen still, waiting for orders. Forward or back, I don't care, but, somewhere, soon, please. It's like being in someone else's nightmare. War is not hell, it's not organized enough to be. Then you come home, if you come home, and get your picture in the paper, mangled in body or spirit. One way or the other, mother, the ghost of your boy is coming home. But not now. Still have some time and life to waste, now. I wonder if the hand is Spanish or American. No such thing as locals here. Just us and other foreigners. Poor people from around the world, shooting each other and wishing we were home. I have to pee so badly. I wonder if you will remember me or think of me, ever. A hungry nobody lying on the ground, watching ants crawling over his leg, trying not to shake, and dying for a single moment of, a single moment of, just a single second where—

Pause. He comes out of his trance.

Okay.

Brief pause.

All right. Good. I think that should...we're good.

ASSISTANT

Okay? Is everything all—

PHOTOGRAPHER

Interrupting.

We're good.

ASSISTANT

So...okay. I guess we're... I guess we're ready.

The following series of lines are all spoken to the audience, most of them very much as if they are gentle "directions" one might give an actor or model whose photo is being taken. Throughout, PHOTOGRAPHER will be looking through the viewfinder, making adjustments, and surveying the audience.

"Bully Composition." Here we go. There you are.

PHOTOGRAPHER

Looking through viewfinder.

There you are.

ASSISTANT

Is it morning or evening?

PHOTOGRAPHER

It's morning.

ASSISTANT

It might be evening.

PHOTOGRAPHER

Making a small adjustment to the camera. Returning to viewfinder.

You're just sitting there. All is quiet.

ASSISTANT

Or is it. Even The Hundred Years' War had a middle. A little quiet moment in the middle that somehow determined the end.

She holds for a moment, to allow for a "quiet little moment."

Like that.

PHOTOGRAPHER

Smoke starts to come out onto the stage. Looking through the viewfinder.

Good. Nice.

Noticing smoke.

I don't know what the smoke is. I think it's for something else. Don't pay any attention. I'm sure it's fine. Just be you.

ASSISTANT

On the threshold of death.

PHOTOGRAPHER

Just act natural.

ASSISTANT

You're sitting on a wooden box. There's a war going on. A real war. The blurry flag gently waves. Maybe you're about to be shot in the throat.

Quietly, plainly:

Bang.

Brief pause.

Splendid.

PHOTOGRAPHER

Good.

Looking through viewfinder.

I think this is good.

He looks again.

It might even be better.

ASSISTANT

It's really… We don't need the other photo. This is it, now. God, if you could see yourselves. So solemn. So divided. What are *you* in the middle of? How do *you* want to be remembered? What are we to see in your eyes?

PHOTOGRAPHER

Just try to sit up nice and straight.

To someone in the audience wearing glasses.

 Maybe you could take your glasses off. Or, no, they're good.

To ASSISTANT:

Keep going.

ASSISTANT

Are you afraid of dying or happy to be alive? The fighting, the horror, the glory, our country—is it over or has it not even started? Show us the national dilemma, in your faces. It's beautiful. Your anxieties, your agonies. They're so photogenic.

PHOTOGRAPHER

Thanks everyone. Almost there.

ASSISTANT

A little more. Nice and gentle. Breathe. Now, feel more things. Think bigger things. This is going to be you, someday. Gorgeous. Wonderful. Be historical.

PHOTOGRAPHER

Good.

To a particular person in the audience, in response to his or her expression.

Very nice, keep that, keep that.

ASSISTANT

Show us you, trying to be better, mortally afraid.

PHOTOGRAPHER

Making adjustments to camera, exposure settings, etc.

Thank you. Last chance. Almost, almost...

ASSISTANT

Be more tragic. More forgiving. More unknowing. More mortal. Try to be more mortal. As much as you can stand.

PHOTOGRAPHER

He looks up from the viewfinder.

Yeah. Perfect.

Camera flash. Blackout.

END

OH, THE HUMANITY

Dramatis Personae

MAN

WOMAN

MAN #2

Setting

Two Chairs.

Stage.

Stage properties

A bottle of water.

Lipstick.

OH, THE HUMANITY

MAN and WOMAN are seated in two chairs, facing the audience. The chairs are arranged as if to be the front seat of a car. There are no other major props and nothing other than stage directions and the actors' gestures to indicate the existence of a car or any of its parts (such as a rearview mirror) onstage. WOMAN is putting on lipstick in the rearview mirror. MAN puts the key into the ignition, turns the key. We hear the sound effect of an engine cranking but not starting. MAN turns key again, same. MAN gets out, goes around to the front, then the back, of the car.

WOMAN

Checking her lipstick, arranging her hair.

Is it the battery?

MAN

No.

WOMAN

What is it? Are we stuck?

MAN

It's just chairs.

WOMAN

What, hon?

MAN

It's just two chairs.

WOMAN

Still arranging her hair, touching up her lipstick.

You're kidding. Just two regular chairs?

MAN

Yeah.

WOMAN

So, how do we get to the church? What time's the christen-ing?

MAN

I thought it was a funeral.

WOMAN

Well, whichever. It was definitely a church. Now we're going to be late.

MAN

Very softly, almost to himself.

I thought it was a funeral.

WOMAN

Darling, let's not fight.

MAN

I'm not fighting. At all. Not at all.

WOMAN

No, of course you're not, I know.

Brief pause.

And even if you were: it's over, thank God. Now, what were you saying?

MAN

I thought my father died and we were going to bury him.

WOMAN

Well, that may well be. It's a busy time.

MAN

What does that mean?

WOMAN

It means, well, just think. Of all the things. All the life beyond our immediate—God, I don't even know—surroundings. Refugees pouring over borders, quintuplets being born, floods in distant countries, meteor showers, mudslides, adultery. Wheat gently blowing in a wheat field somewhere, an animal being put to sleep. Great moments in sports, boat shows, volcanoes, tornadoes, grandmothers being wheeled into nursing homes, never to see natural light again. Think of it all. God. What a busy world. Such a busy time.

She drinks from a bottle of water. Brief pause.

Medical breakthroughs, personal setbacks, embarrassing moments in literature. Millions of things. War, famine, misunderstanding. Car trouble. Simple pain in everyday settings.

Brief pause.

Boat shows. I already said that.

MAN is staring off, perhaps in mourning.

MAN

He was just mowing the lawn, yesterday.

WOMAN

She continues on.

Whales washing up on empty beaches. Home-pregnancy test kits being thrown through windows. Anniversaries, coronations, cremations, and parades. Of course, there's more, but, I'm done. Oh, and my niece being christened. And don't forget your father, his glasses sideways on his face, going to his knees in the half-cut grass, pointing at his mouth.

MAN

Brief pause.

I would like it if we could leave here. I'm going to take another look

He goes around to the back of the car.

WOMAN

Turning and resting an arm on the backs of the chairs.

Anything?

MAN

Again...

He gestures toward the chairs.

WOMAN

Ah, yes. Our predicament.

MAN

Is that what this is?

WOMAN

It's a word, okay? It describes something. So what do we do?

MAN #2

Enters. Stands quietly to the side. MAN and WOMAN notice him, but are not overly concerned with his arrival or his presence.

MAN

Lost in thought. Sadly.

My father. To his knees, like that? His glasses sideways on his face? Do you think?

WOMAN

Maybe.

MAN

And your niece?

WOMAN

Smiling, crying, reaching for something. Saliva bubbling out of her mouth. Or that's your dad. It's quite a world.

MAN

And here we are, missing it. Late for it.

Brief pause.

You know, I'm really trying. I am. To be—I don't know—to be something, to be truthful somehow, sitting here in my chair, with you, and that other chair. I'm starting to–. This is so–. I'm going to miss him. I'm really trying here. Here, in our little–.

Brief pause.

The eagle does not try. The mouse does not try. But is the eagle not in fact the mouse?

WOMAN

No.

MAN

But you get my point.

WOMAN

No.

MAN

No, okay. But, do you see a larger mystery?

WOMAN

Do I see a different mystery? Do I see stranger relations—
between things and *not* between things, do I sense a wider
deeper sense of wonder and mayhem? Do I feel a whole set
of simple established facts missing, the rug disintegrating
thread-by-thread, gone before it can even be pulled out from
underneath us?

MAN

Yes.

WOMAN

I do. I think I do.

MAN

Because I'm starting to wonder.

WOMAN

To MAN #2:

Do you know anything about cars?

MAN #2

Oh. No. I mean, I know that they're convenient.

WOMAN

Who are you?

MAN #2

It's a little embarrassing. You're probably going to laugh. But, I'm the beauty of things, the majesty of—I don't know—the world? The Universe? Although, just to let you know, I don't possess any secret knowledge or any glimpse into anything, so, I wouldn't bother to, you know…

MAN and WOMAN return their attentions to each other.

MAN

To WOMAN.

Because, like I said, I'm starting to wonder. To wonder, and, struggle a little, here. In our world in which so much is happening, reportedly.

WOMAN

Checking her watch.

We should almost be there.

MAN

Quietly.

Where?

WOMAN

Checking her watch.

We're definitely late.

MAN

I'm trying. I am, so hard. To make the best of this. To not just start shouting. To not start hating you just because I'm afraid and I don't understand. Or start crying. I'm trying, Vanessa.

Pause. He is almost crying, though managing to cover it, to control himself.

But, these are chairs. And I don't know where… I don't know what we're supposed to do. And I want my father. I miss my dad. There's some stranger standing here. And these are chairs. And that's it. And I don't know who I am.

WOMAN

There there.

Pause.

Isn't that awful? How far can you push a person away, with just two words? "There there."

MAN

Very brief pause.

That's it?

WOMAN

What? People expect people to be so loving in these situations.

MAN

"These situations?"

WOMAN

I don't know. How am I supposed to know? You think I'm not trying, too? You, me, and two stupid chairs—and you're so surprised that I haven't made a more stable, more substantial, more loving life for myself, for us? I thought we were going to a christening. Maybe a baptism. The little baby, all in white, waiting for a name. Some incense, some soothing inscrutable Latin, a chance to see everyone. A ritual, any ritual, just something to take pictures of. A Bat Mitzvah or a Hindu Naming Ceremony, I don't care. I had one tiny wish. Let's go somewhere and see something. An innocent beginning or a gruesome end, anything. But, alas, it seems, No.

MAN

I'm trying to picture him. Whatever suit they put him in.

WOMAN

Her little hands and those big eyes, looking up, or, asleep. As they say prayers for her name or whatever they do. Her mouth a little mess of saliva.

MAN

His glasses on, nice and straight. Him all dressed up. Everyone there.

WOMAN

And the sunlight through the stained-glass windows. Everyone there. The otherworldly music.

MAN

All the skinny undertakers, outside, smoking. Him all dry, all preserved. He was mowing the lawn, yesterday. Bye, Dad.

WOMAN

Katie is a pretty name. I do love their little hands and the great big eyes. Katie, maybe. It'd be nice if they decided on "Katie."

MAN #2

From where he has been standing, MAN #2 begins speaking to the audience.

It would probably come as no surprise to you were I to suddenly move closer to you, now.

He does not move.

It would come as no surprise, I'm sure, were I to suddenly begin my speech, to bring it all home, as we all move closer and closer. All of us certain of simple things, certain in our knowledge that we are loved, that people love us, that God loves us, that God exists and loves us, that people exist and love us.

A general pause.

I can see from your faces. That that would come as no surprise. For me to do something very expected like that.

Brief pause.

Ah. Your faces. So fragile, so certain. The majesty.

Lights fade.

END

OTHER WILL ENO TITLES

Middletown
ISBN 9781849430661

Title and Deed
ISBN 9781849434805

Thom Pain (based on nothing)
ISBN 9781840024524

The Flu Season
ISBN 9781840023701

Tragedy: a tragedy
ISBN 9781840022346

WWW.OBERONBOOKS.COM